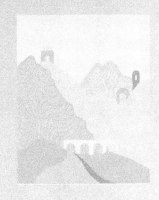

FASCINATING LANDSCAPES

Adult Coloring Book for Relaxation and Stress Relief

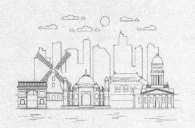
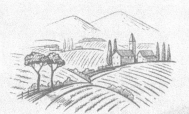

Nature & Art Editions

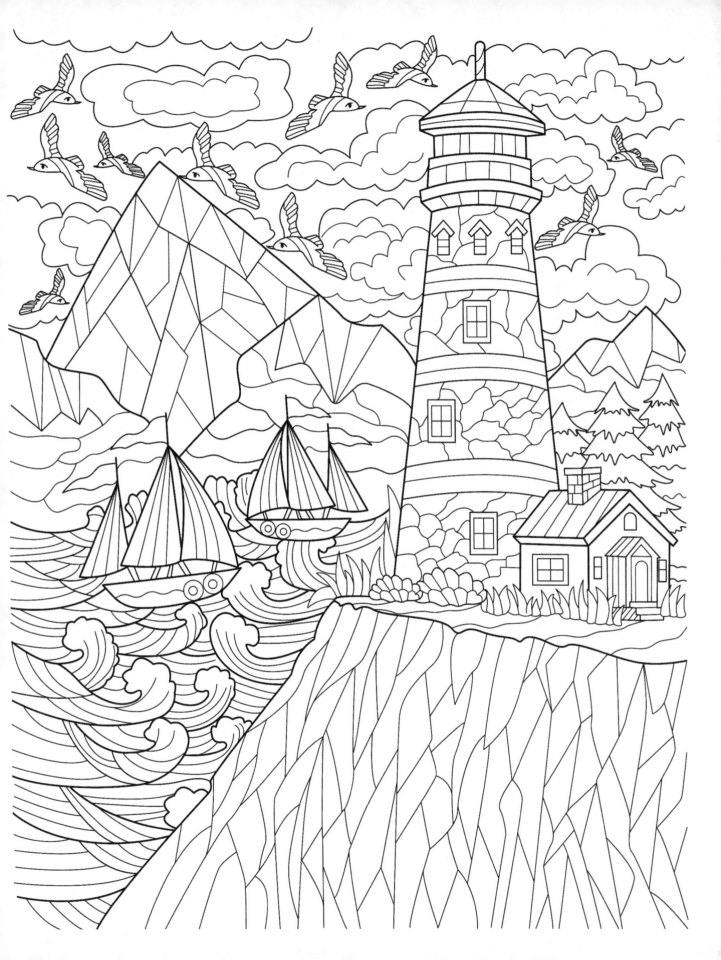

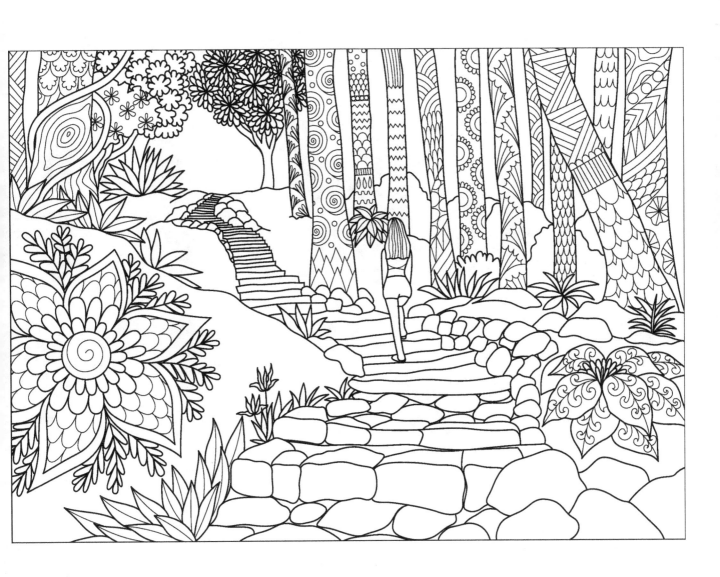

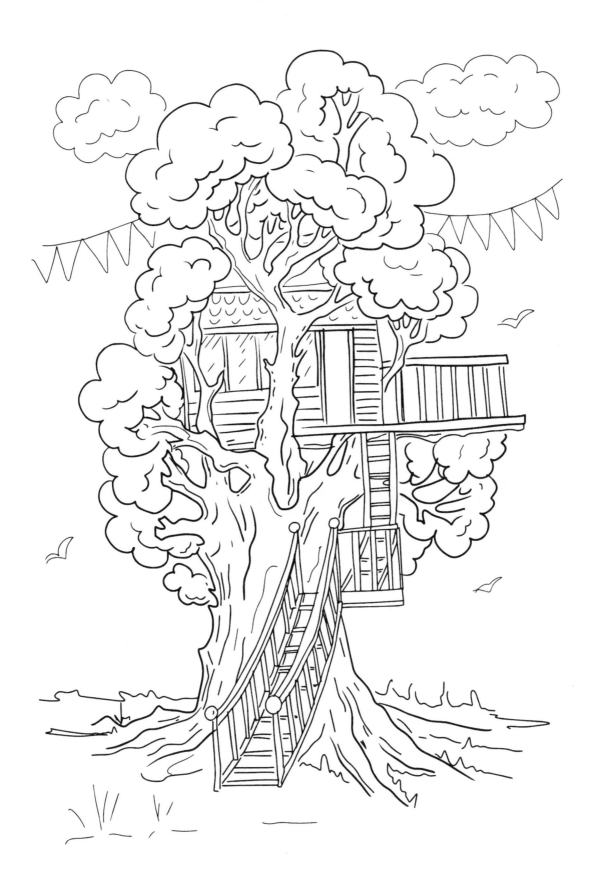

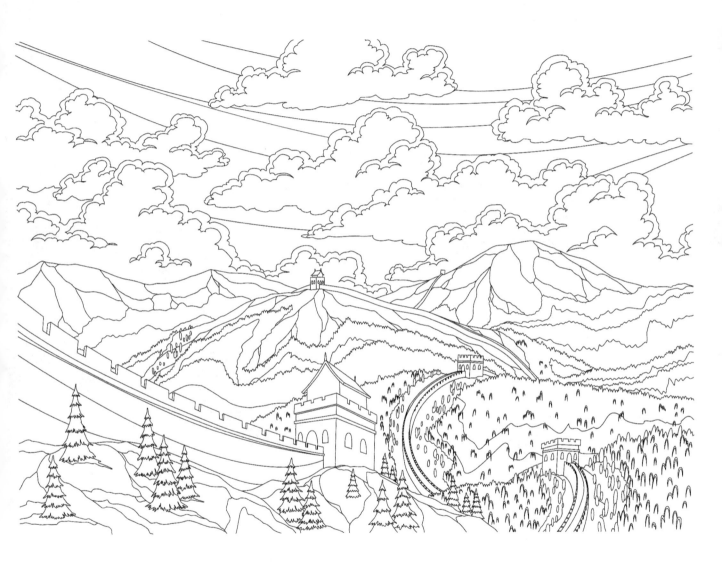

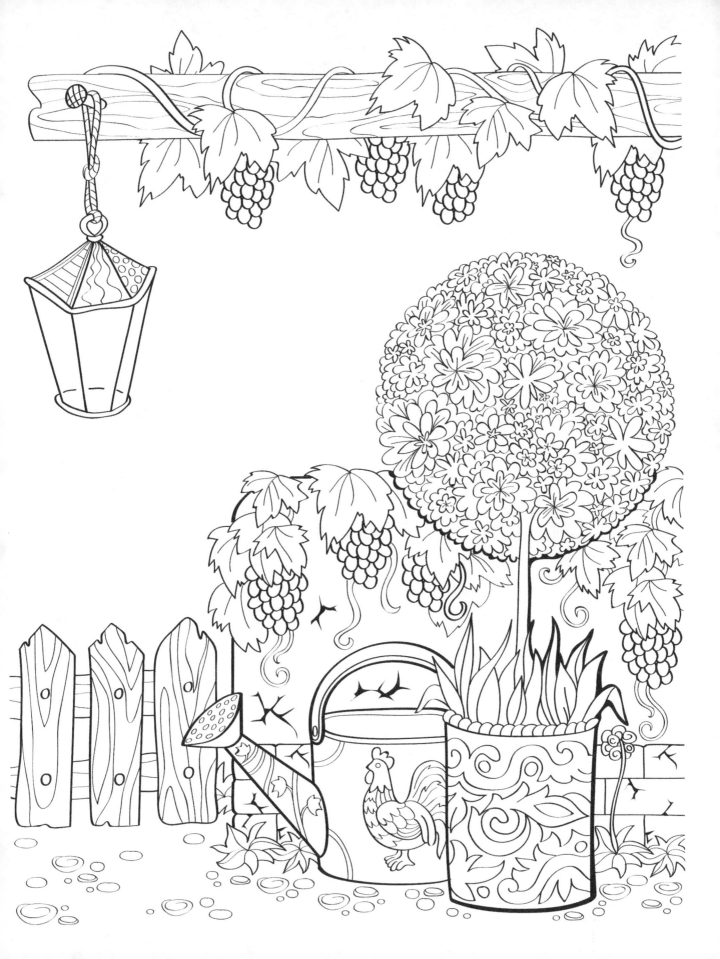

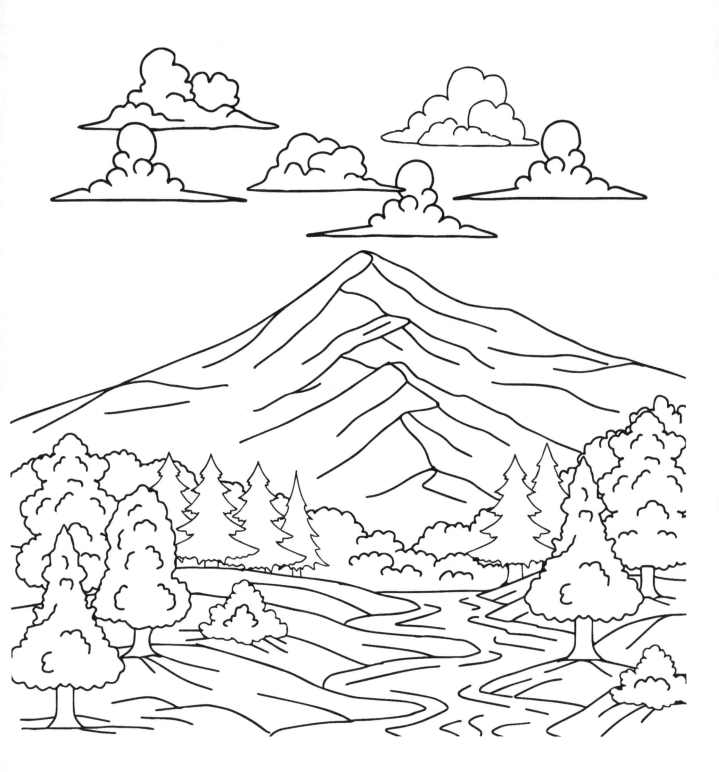

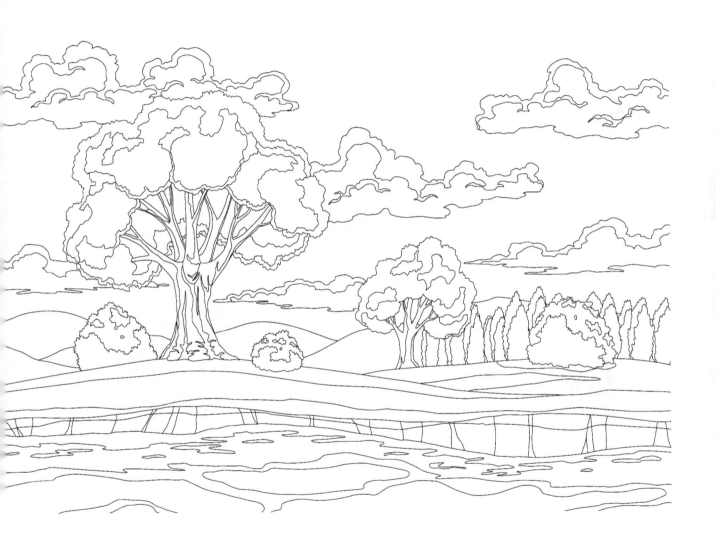

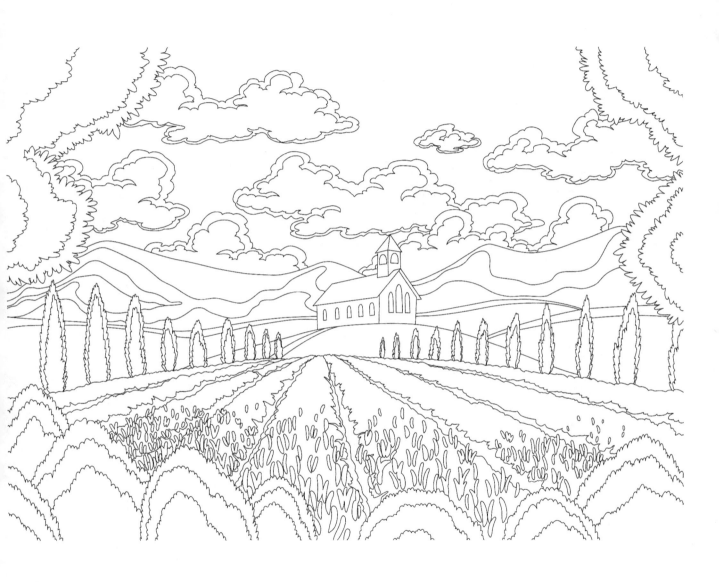

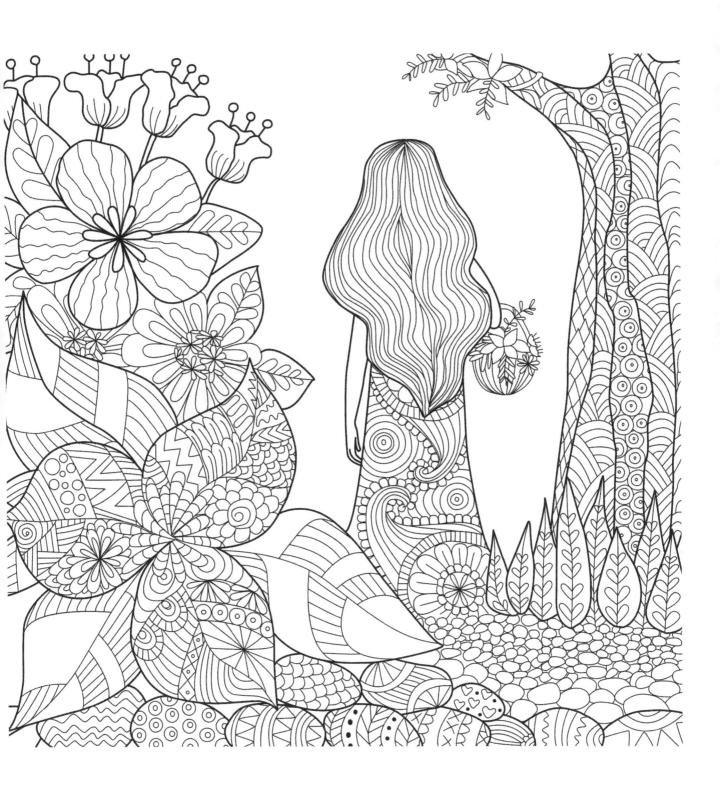

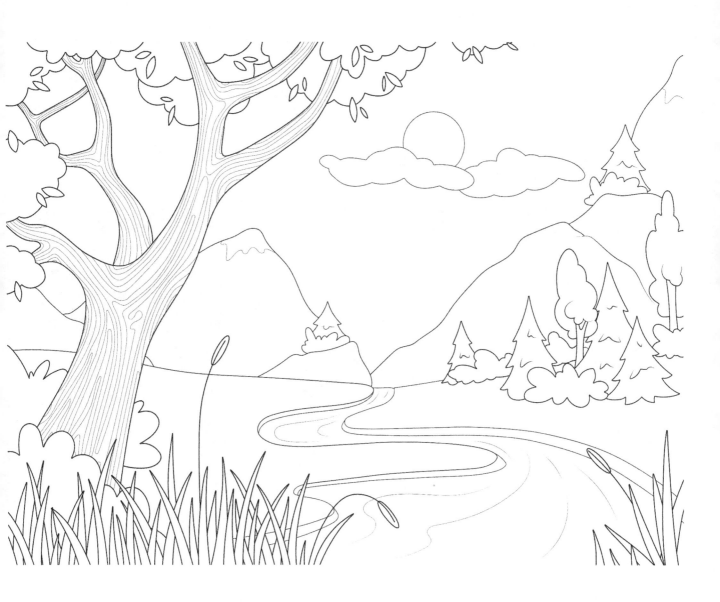

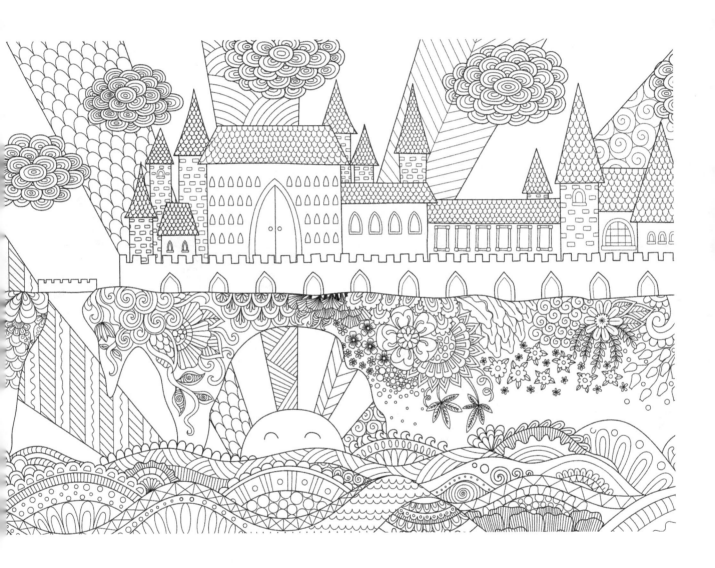

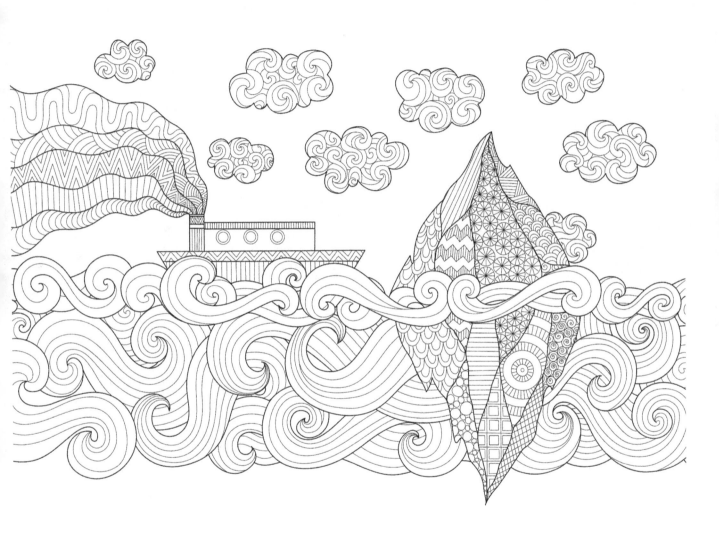

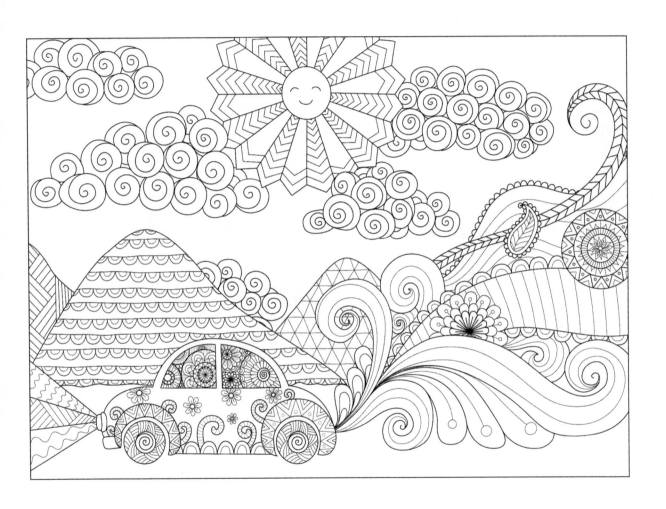

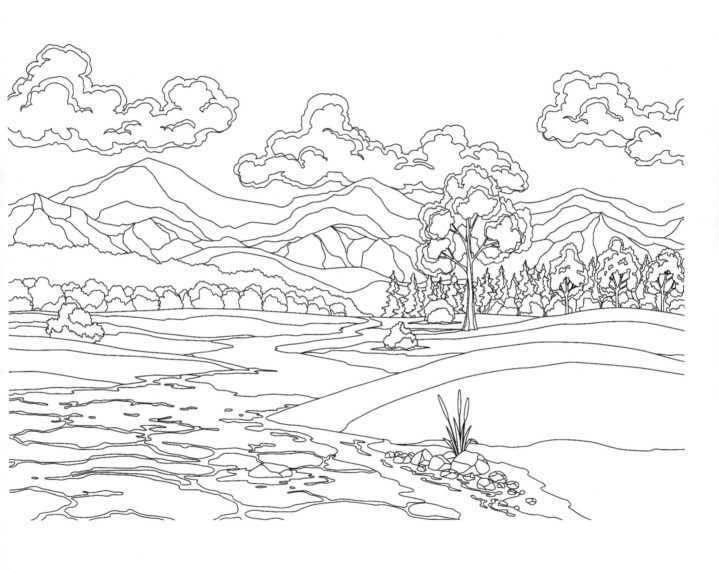

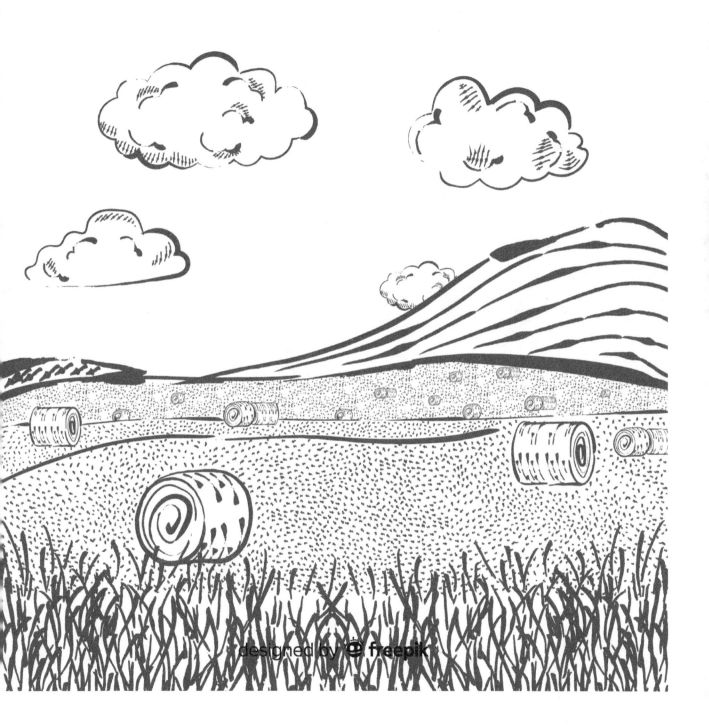

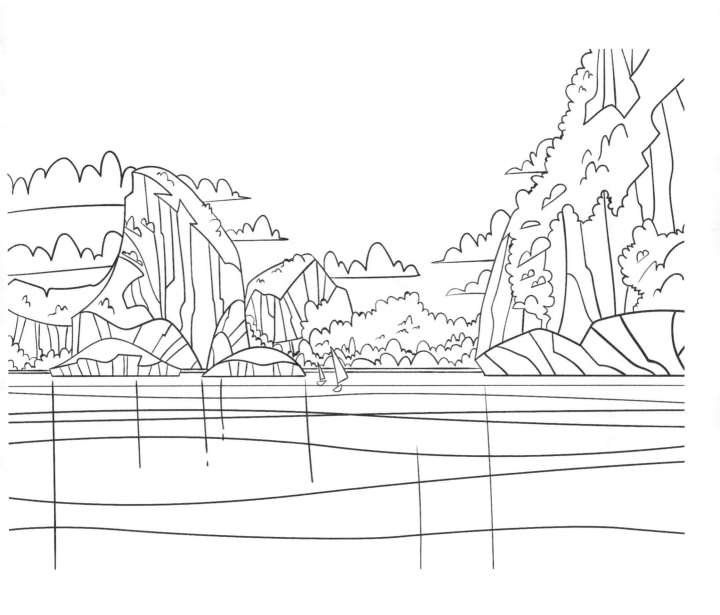

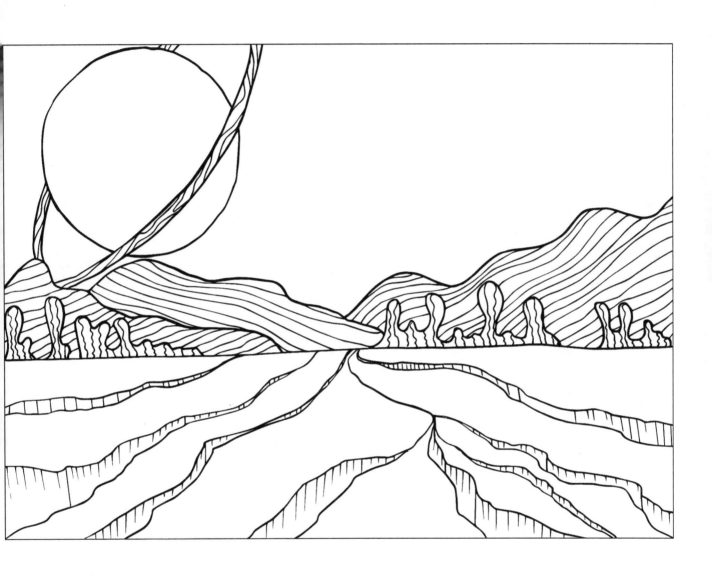

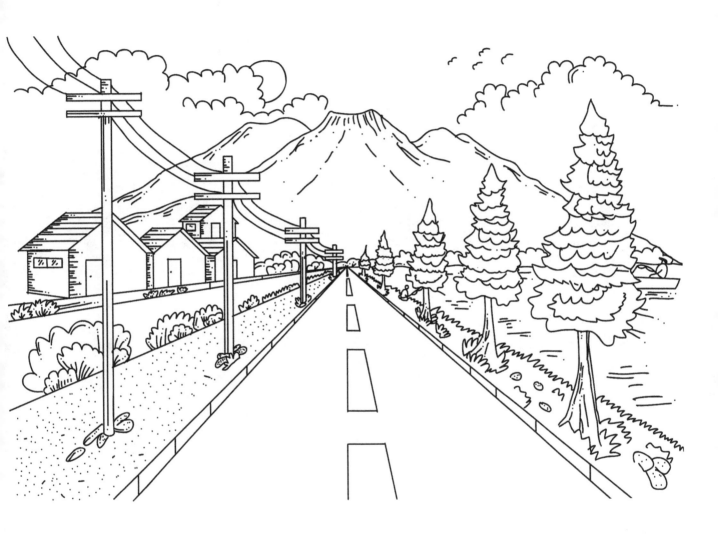

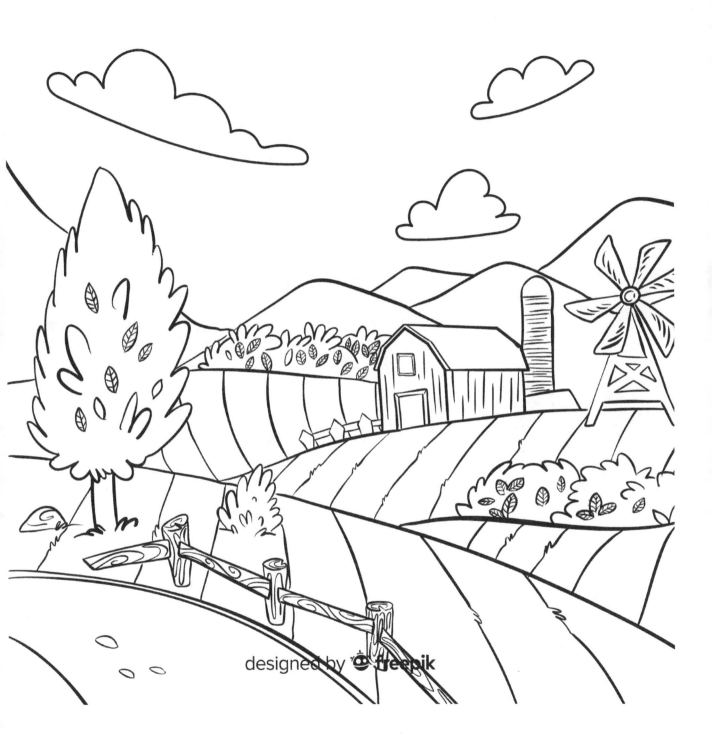

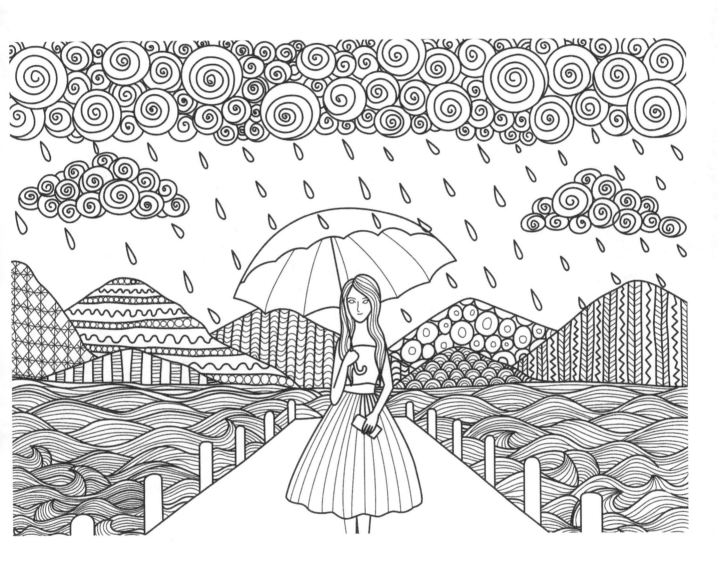

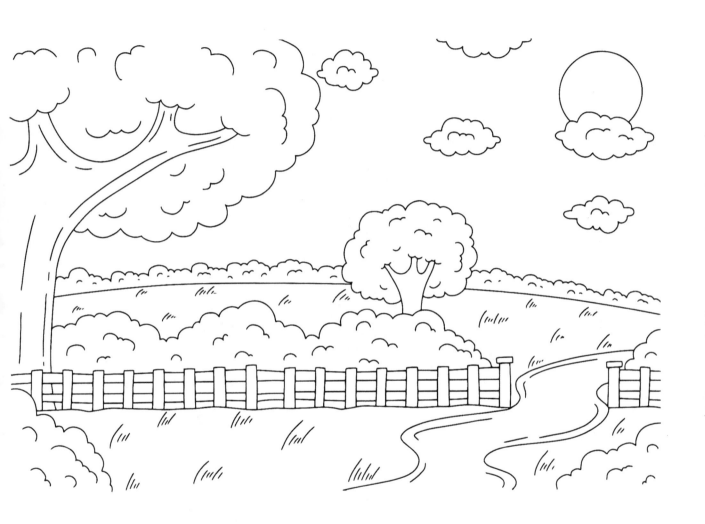

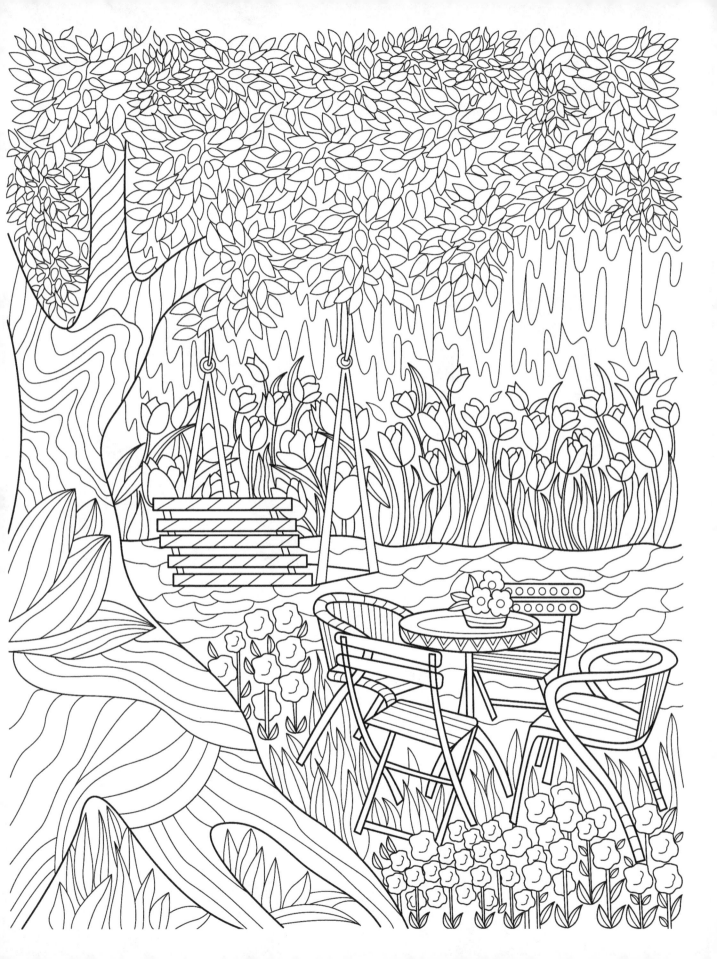

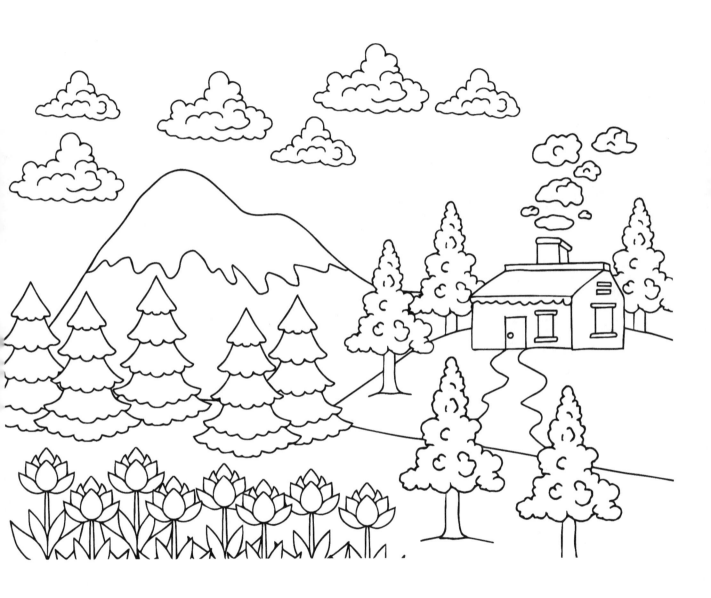

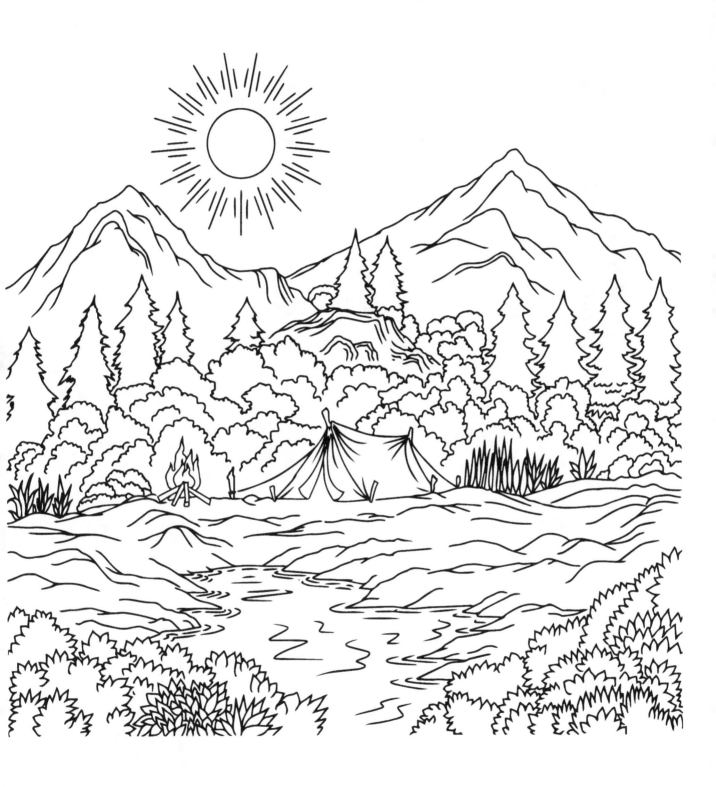

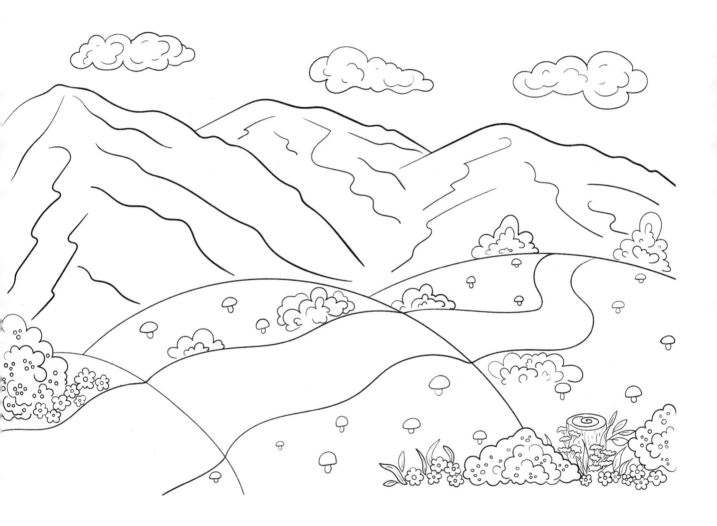

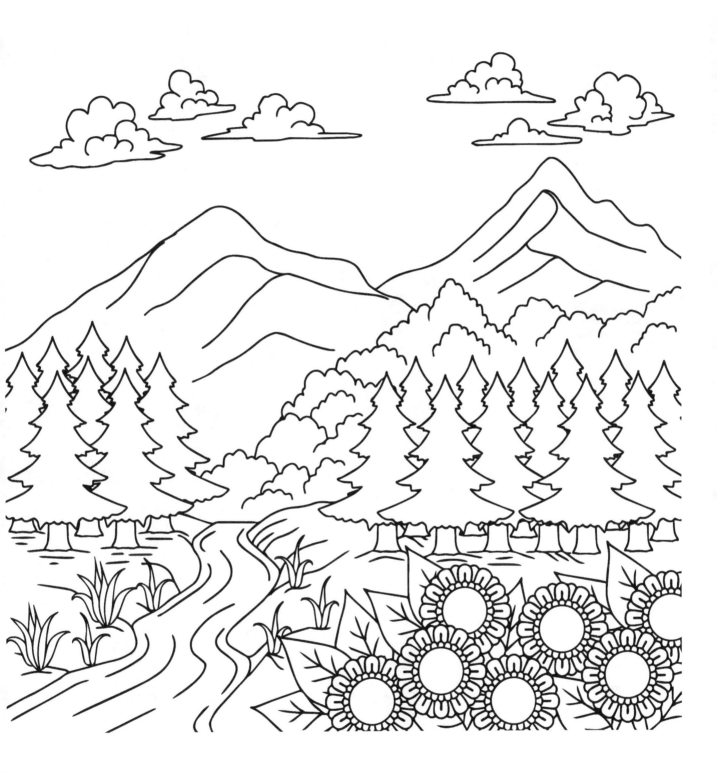

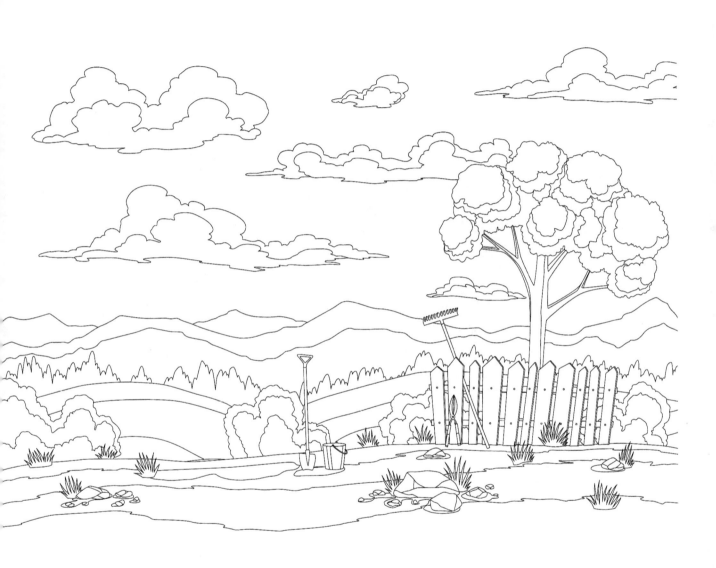

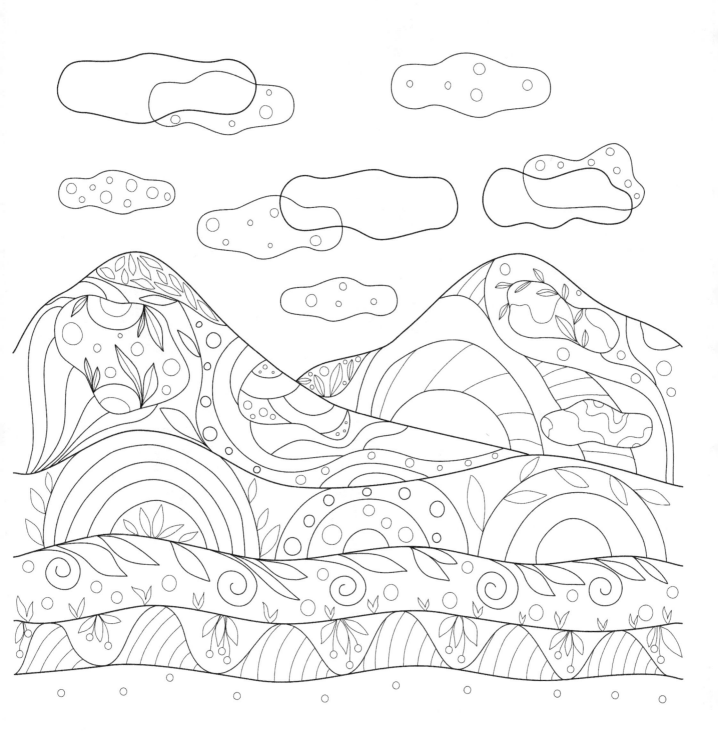

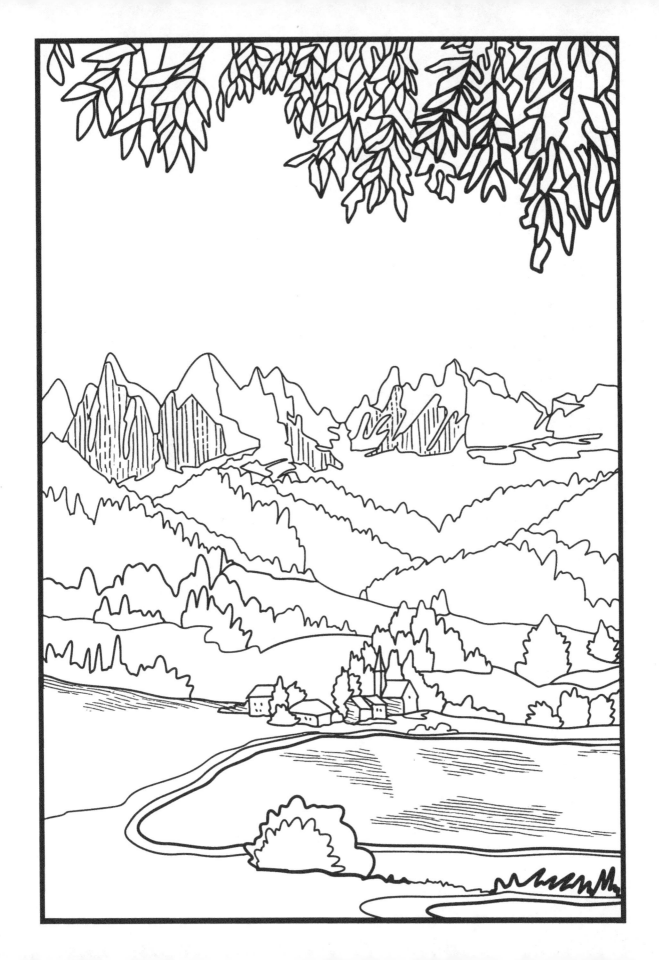

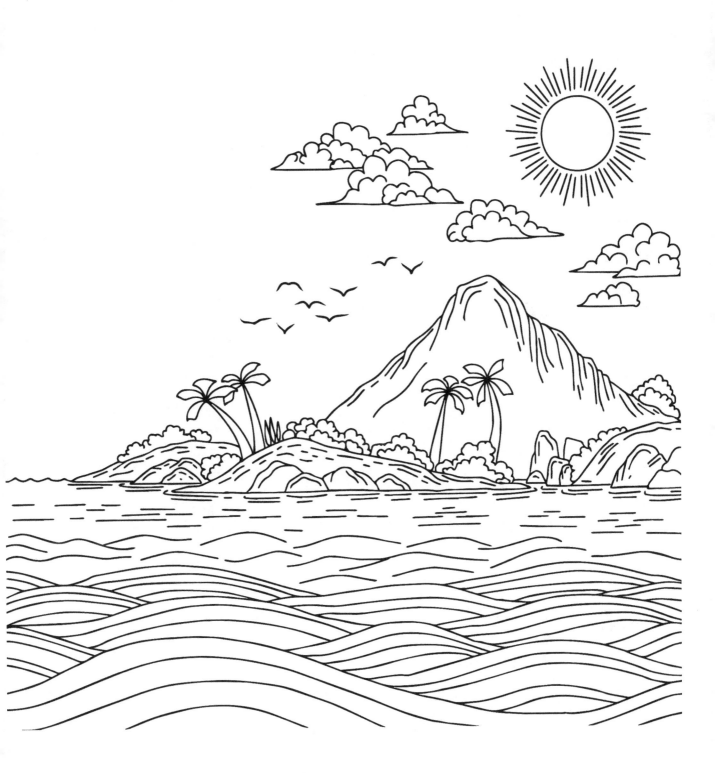

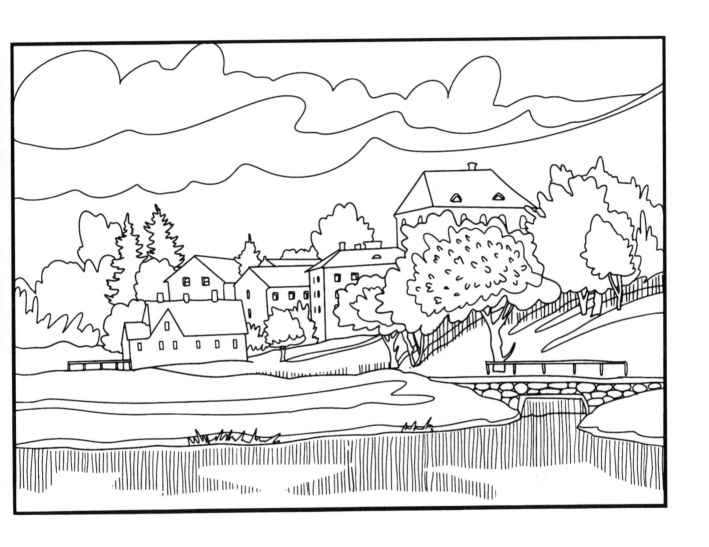

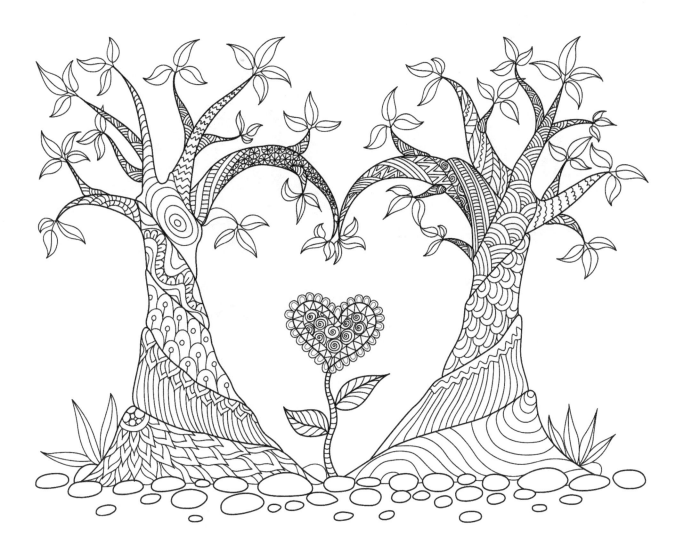

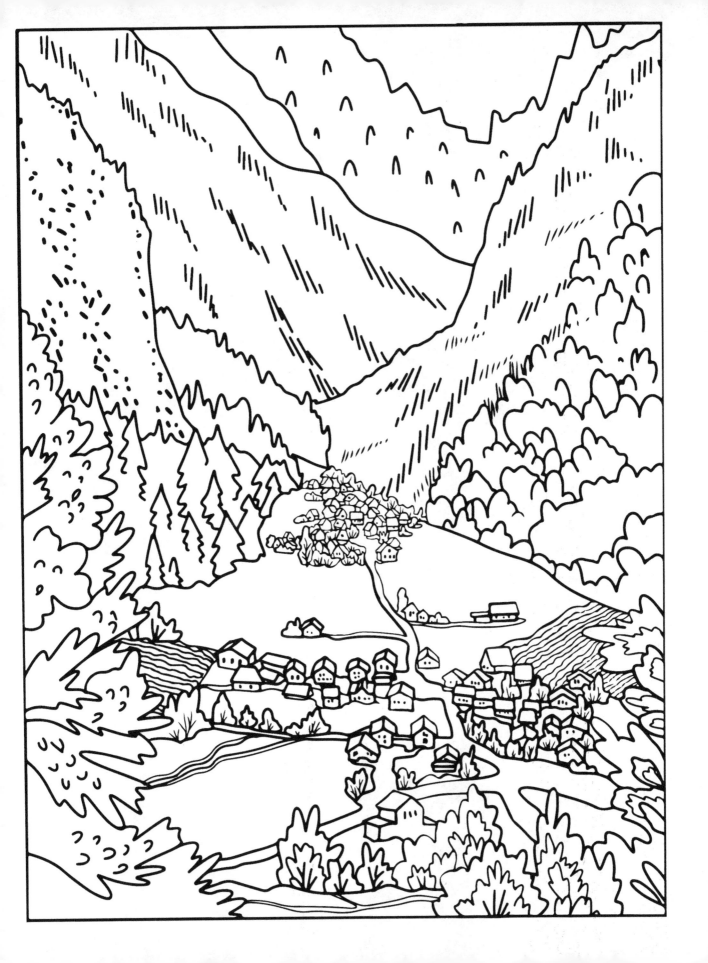

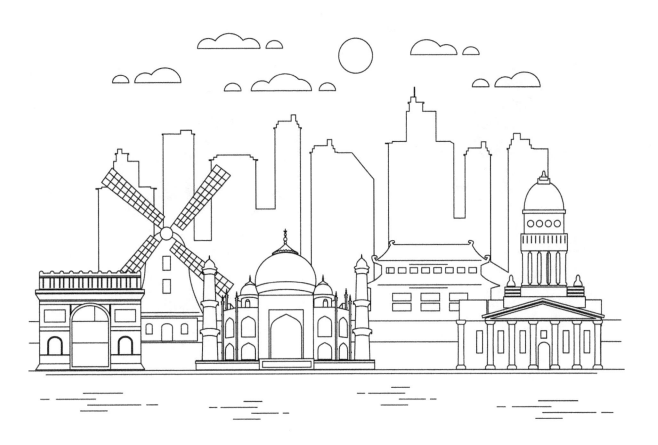

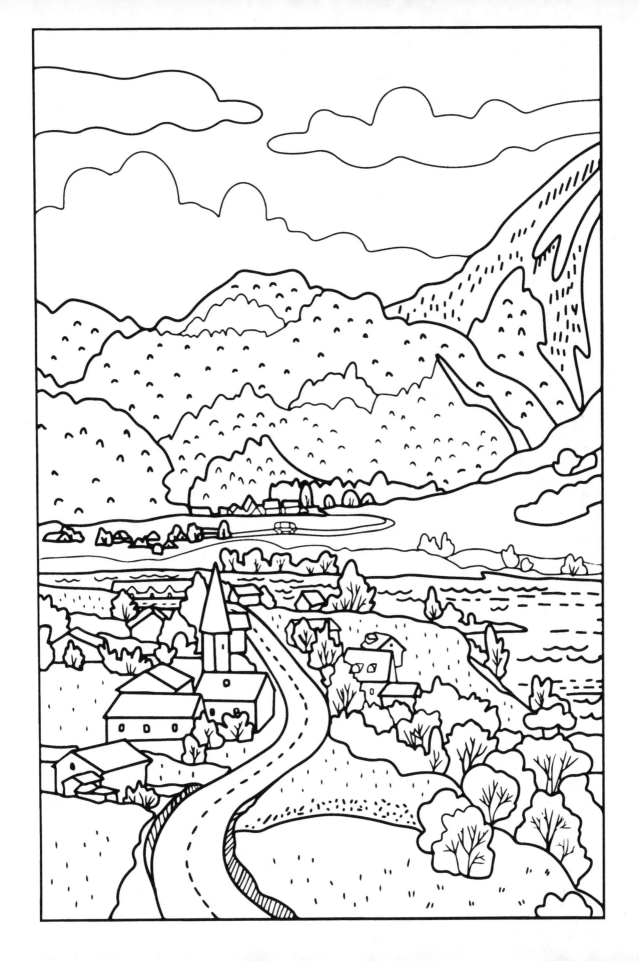

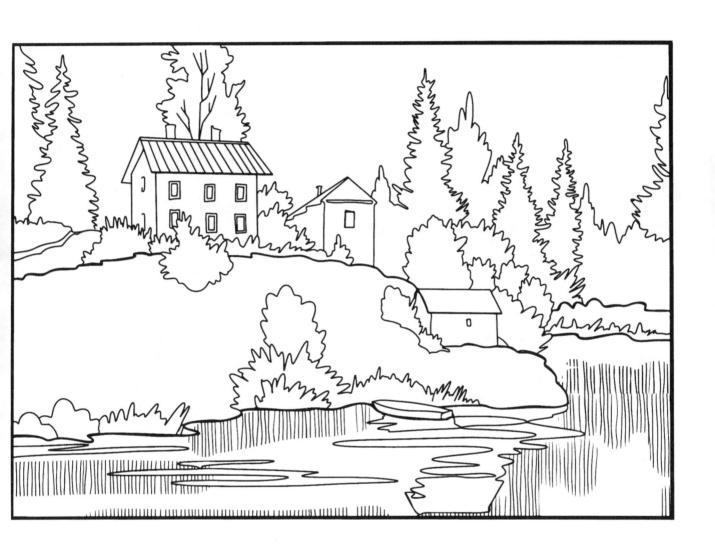

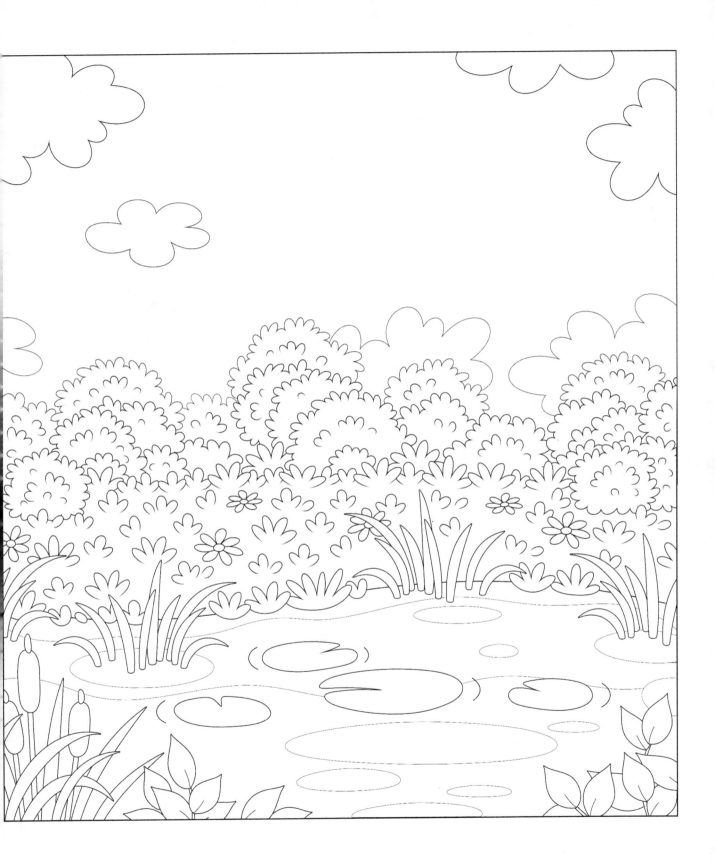

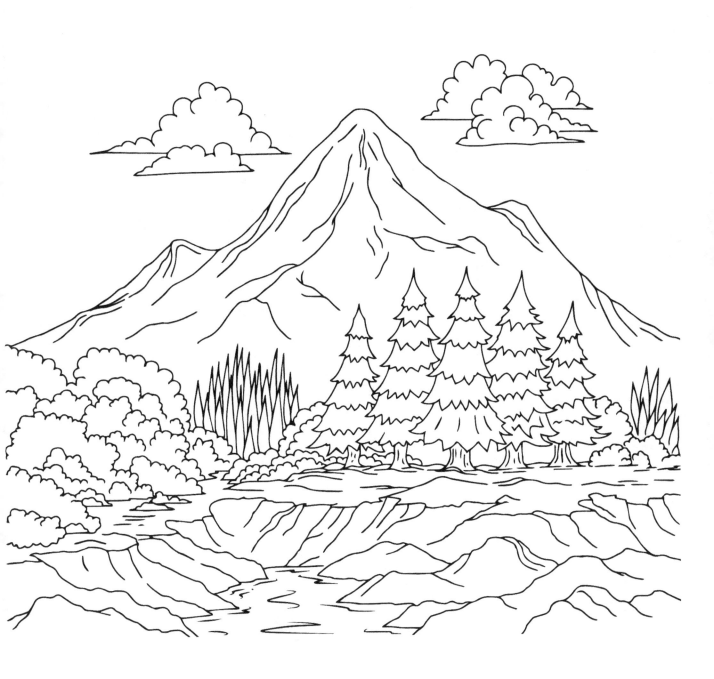

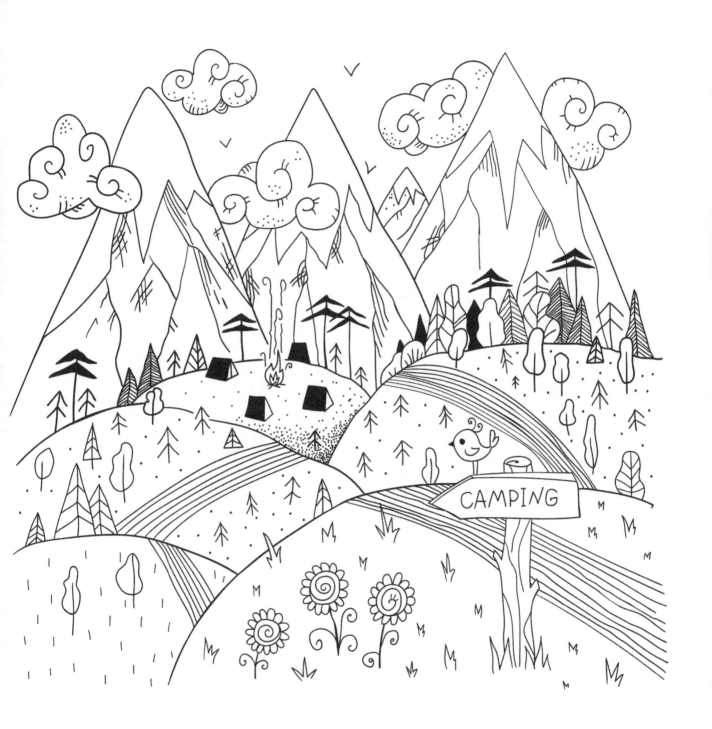

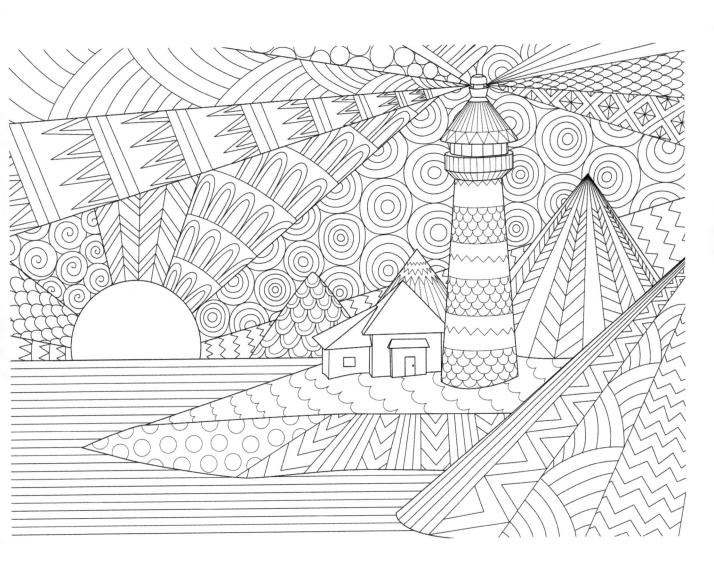

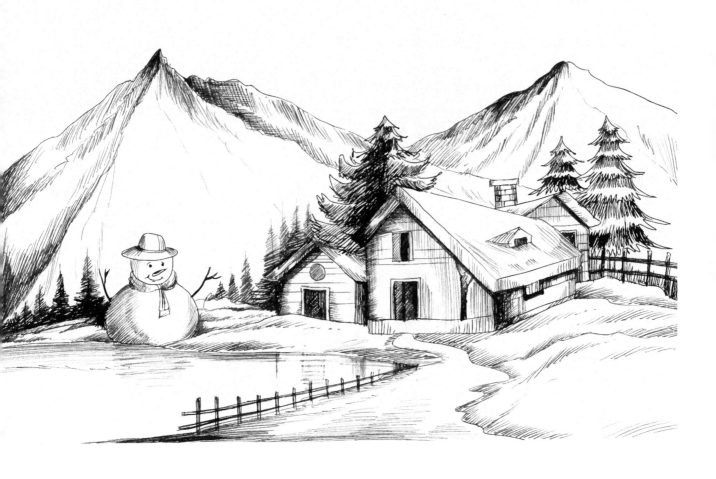

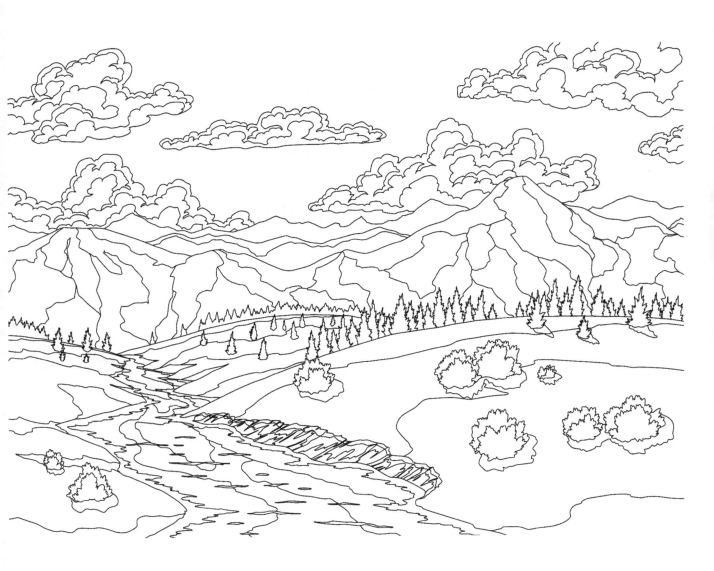

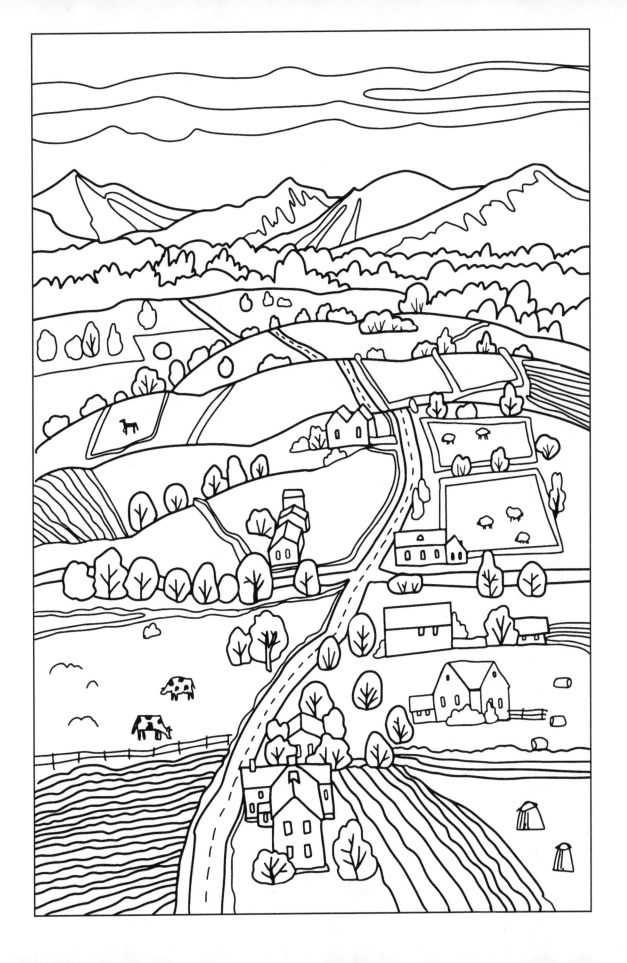

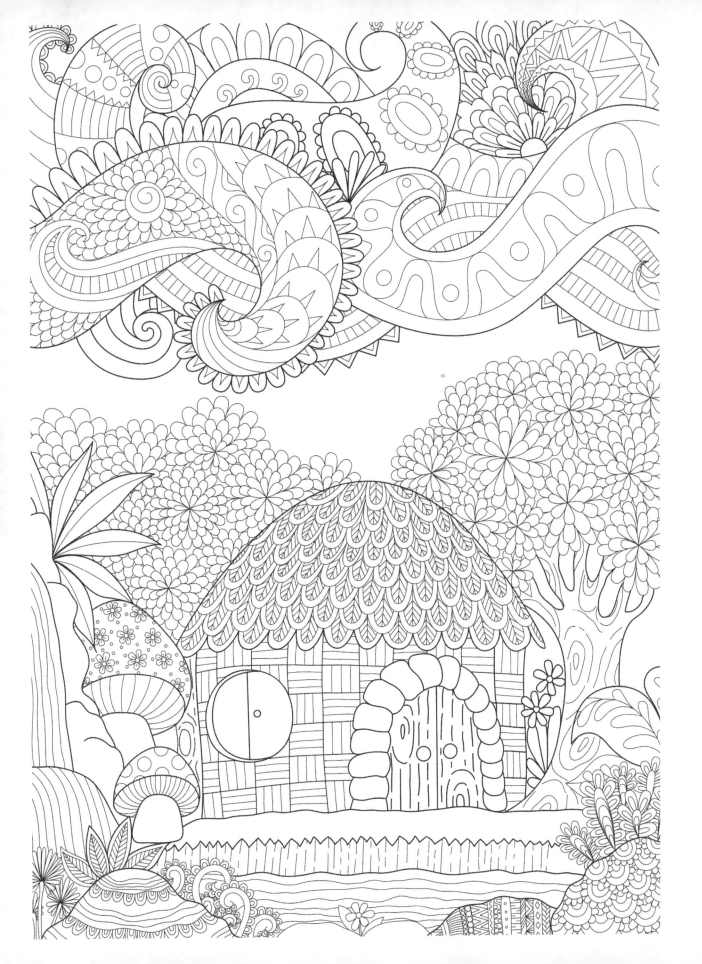

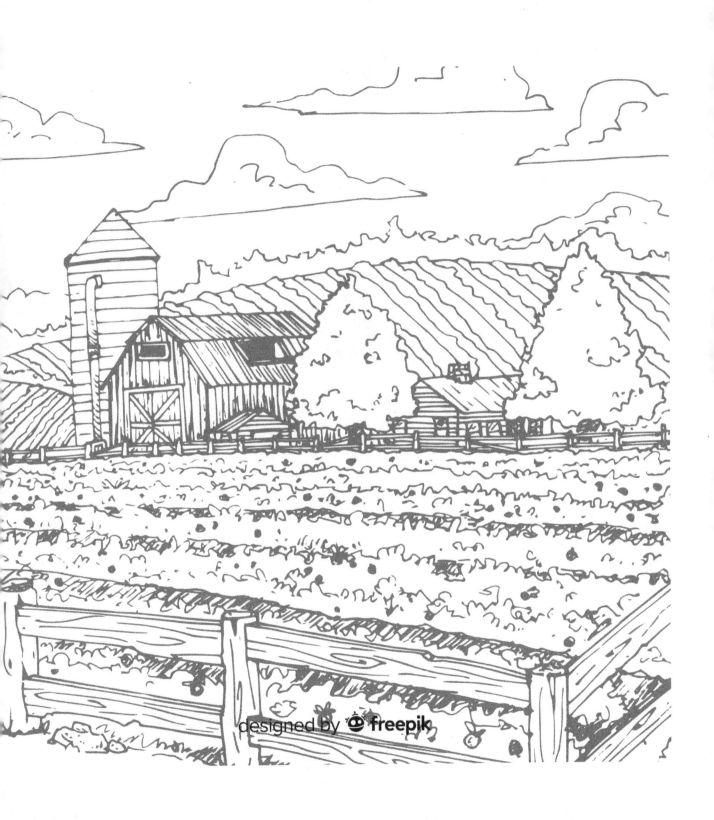

CPSIA information can be obtained
at www.ICGtesting.com
Printed in the USA
BVHW021519130423
662292BV00012B/450